Daniel
Set Apart and Sent

Published by CruPress®
crustore.org
CruPress
7157 Narcoosee Rd. #1221
Orlando, FL 32822

Written by Brian Barnett
Adapted from a prior Cru study by Tim Henderson
Edited by Rick James
Copyedited by Elisabeth Thoresen
Designed by Julie Plasse

CruPress is the publishing ministry of Cru®.

Additional copies:
crustore.org
1-800-827-2788

ISBN number: 978-1-57334-232-2

All Scripture quotations, unless otherwise indicated, are taken from the Holy Bible, New International Version®, NIV®. Copyright ©1973, 1978, 1984, 2011 by Biblica, Inc.™ Used by permission of Zondervan. All rights reserved worldwide. www.zondervan.com The "NIV" and "New International Version" are trademarks registered in the United States Patent and Trademark Office by Biblica, Inc.™

Scripture quotations marked ESV are from the ESV® Bible (The Holy Bible, English Standard Version®), copyright © 2001 by Crossway, a publishing ministry of Good News Publishers. Used by permission. All rights reserved. The ESV text may not be quoted in any publication made available to the public by a Creative Commons license. The ESV may not be translated into any other language.

© 2023 Cru Press, Cru. All rights reserved. No part of this publication may be reproduced, stored in a retrieval system, or transmitted in any form or by any means, including photocopying, recording, or other electronic or mechanical methods, without the prior permission of Cru Press.

Contents

Introduction 3
Daniel 1 5
Daniel 2 14
Daniel 3 25
Daniel 4 34
Daniel 5 44
Daniel 6 54
Daniel 7 64

Introduction

Have you wondered how to live as a Christian in a challenging, secular, and materialist world? Have you desired to live set apart for Christ, while also being sent by Christ to engage the world in an authentic way about Christ? Have you desired to live in Christian community, while not living exclusively in a self-affirming Christian bubble? Have you wanted to be an authentic believer living in a real world? Well...the book of Daniel was written, in part, as an example for just these reasons. That's right, a book written approximately 2,500 years ago speaks clearly to the reality we are facing today as Christians in this world!

Daniel was written to be a testimony to the sovereignty, enduring glory, and power of God. Daniel and his friends were able to make that glory known in an entirely secular environment amongst non-believers. Despite being taken from their land, brought into slavery, and likely feeling abandoned by God—Daniel and his friends pursued God, pursued holiness, and proclaimed God to their captors. Through their example, there is much for modern Christians to emulate. More importantly, there is much we can learn from this Old Testament book about the power of God, His love for all people, His amazingly glorious character, and the coming reality of our Savior and King Jesus Christ.

We will study chapters 1-6 to find an astounding narrative of Daniel and his friends living sent by God into a foreign and ungodly land. We'll see how they pursued a relationship with God, while also dramatically proclaiming the salvation of God with humility and boldness. This will result in radically altering the spiritual journey of one anti-God king and many other lives. Finally, we'll look to the future by studying one of the apocalyptic sections of the book of Daniel in chapter 7. We will, rightfully so, end by considering the Messiah, Jesus Christ, Eternal Life, and how this reality should affect the way we currently live.

Much like what Jewish believers experienced in the book of Daniel, God has designed you to be *set apart* by God to live a life of faith and holiness. Simultaneously, God wants to *send* you into this world to proclaim the excellencies of God to the people around you. Jesus' prayer for his followers in John 17 is modeled by the followers of God in the book of Daniel and it is my hope for you: "My prayer is not that you take them out of the world but that you protect them from the evil one. They are *not of the world*, even as I am not of it. Sanctify them by the truth; your word is truth. As you sent me into the world, I have *sent them into the world*" (John 17:15-18, italics mine).

Brian Barnett
Cru Team Leader, Tidewater Area
November 2021

Daniel 1

¹In the third year of the reign of Jehoiakim king of Judah, Nebuchadnezzar king of Babylon came to Jerusalem and besieged it. ²And the Lord delivered Jehoiakim king of Judah into his hand, along with some of the articles from the temple of God. These he carried off to the temple of his god in Babylonia and put in the treasure house of his god.

³Then the king ordered Ashpenaz, chief of his court officials, to bring into the king's service some of the Israelites from the royal family and the nobility—⁴young men without any physical defect, handsome, showing aptitude for every kind of learning, well informed, quick to understand, and qualified to serve in the king's palace. He was to teach them the language and literature of the Babylonians. ⁵The king assigned them a daily amount of food and wine from the king's table. They were to be trained for three years, and after that they were to enter the king's service.

⁶Among those who were chosen were some from Judah: Daniel, Hananiah, Mishael and Azariah. ⁷The chief official gave them new names: to Daniel, the name Belteshazzar; to Hananiah, Shadrach; to Mishael, Meshach; and to Azariah, Abednego. ⁸But Daniel resolved not to defile himself with the royal food and wine, and he asked the chief official for permission not to defile himself this way.

⁹Now God had caused the official to show favor and compassion to Daniel, ¹⁰but the official told Daniel, "I am afraid of my lord the king, who has assigned your food and drink. Why should he see you looking worse than the other young men your age? The king would then have my head because of you."

¹¹Daniel then said to the guard whom the chief official had appointed over Daniel, Hananiah, Mishael and Azariah, ¹²"Please test your servants for ten days: Give us nothing but vegetables to eat and water to drink. ¹³Then compare our appearance with that of the young men who eat the royal food, and treat your servants in accordance with what you see." ¹⁴So he agreed to this and tested them for ten days.

¹⁵At the end of the ten days they looked healthier and better nourished than any of the young men who ate the royal food. ¹⁶So the guard took away their choice food and the wine they were to drink and gave them vegetables instead.

¹⁷To these four young men God gave knowledge and understanding of all kinds of literature and learning. And Daniel could understand visions and dreams of all kinds.

¹⁸At the end of the time set by the king to bring them into his service, the chief official presented them to Nebuchadnezzar. ¹⁹The king talked with them, and he found none equal to Daniel, Hananiah, Mishael and Azariah; so they entered the king's service. ²⁰In every matter of wisdom and understanding about which the king questioned them, he found them ten times better than all the magicians and enchanters in his whole kingdom.

²¹And Daniel remained there until the first year of King Cyrus.

Introduction

Daniel is a prophetic book centered around four followers of God who lived out their faith in some extremely difficult situations. It's important to understand the context in which they lived in order to better understand how they followed God and proclaimed God's message. The book of Daniel opens with a brief account of how God's people were taken into captivity by Babylon, an evil and anti-God nation.

It was a shocking and heart-breaking experience for the Jewish people to be overtaken by an ungodly nation. It likely rocked (maybe destroyed) the faith of many believers, but it was also in this context that Daniel and his friends deeply committed and connected to God. The first chapter of Daniel doesn't give much context on this, but the events at the end of 2 Chronicles immediately precede chapter one of Daniel. Let's consider both to better understand the context. Then, let's consider the implications of the actions of Daniel and his friends and how it affects our view of God and how we are to live today.

Discussion Questions

1. When have you spent time in a foreign country or different culture than your own? What emotions did you have when faced with the differences in culture, language, food, traditions, norms, etc.?

Read vv. 1-8.

2. What is the background information we learn about God's people at this time? Who are the Babylonians? Who allowed or caused God's people to be taken into captivity?

3. Read 2 Chronicles 36:15-21 for more background information. What do you learn about God from these verses? Why were the people of God put into exile through the overtaking of the Babylonians?

4. What kind of emotions do you think the Jewish people are feeling in captivity? How would you imagine Daniel, Hananiah, Mishael, and Azariah are feeling toward God?

5. In the Jewish custom, names held significant meaning and purpose. Why do you think Daniel and his friends accept having their names changed, but do not accept eating the royal food and wine?

6. *Apply:* What things have you had to refuse or give up in order to walk more closely with God? What things do you need to refuse or change in your life to walk more with God?

Read vv. 9-21

7. How did Daniel approach and interact with the Babylonian guards and officials? Considering the circumstances, why is this especially outstanding?

8. What kind of "test" does Daniel ask to have? What are the results?

9. How do you see God working "behind the scenes" in this story? How does God help these godly men spiritually, but also practically?

10. *Apply:* In the last month, how have you personally seen God working on your behalf and helping you in your day-to-day life?

11. How were Daniel and his friends being used as examples and messengers of God?

12. If God really was sending Daniel and his friends into the Babylonian world to proclaim the glory of God, why do you think there is no indication that Daniel or his friends spoke about God during their three years of training time?

13. *Apply:* Verse 17 says, "God gave [them] knowledge and understanding of all kinds…" How do we see this promise fulfilled in Jesus? (Hint: Look at Colossians 2:2-3) Do you experience this in your life daily?

Read John 17:15-18

14. Summarize Jesus' prayer for His followers. How did Daniel and his friends model these commands?

15. *Apply:* What does it mean to be sanctified by the truth? Daniel was careful to not do anything to defile himself before God—in what areas do you need God to sanctify you?

16. *Apply:* Jesus says, "As you sent me into the world, I have sent them into the world." How do you need to view yourself more as being sent by God into this world? What steps do you need to take to more practically represent Jesus in the places God has put you in?

Considerations and Synopsis

The book of Daniel opens with a brief account of how Judah (God's chosen nation) was taken into captivity by Babylon. The important thing to understand is that God was judging Judah. By allowing a wicked nation to subdue them, in response to years of Jewish sin and idolatry, His judgement was both swift and dumbfounding for many Jews. However, this was warned of by the prophets repeatedly. To further understand the reasons behind this captivity and why God allowed this to happen, look at the end of Second Chronicles. The book of Daniel picks up immediately following the events of 2 Chronicles 36:15-17:

> "The LORD, the God of their ancestors, sent word to them through his messengers again and again, because he had pity on his people and on his dwelling place. But they mocked God's messengers, despised his words and scoffed at his prophets until the wrath of the LORD was aroused against his people and there was no remedy. He brought up against them the king of the Babylonians…"

God tried and tried again to get his people to turn back to him, but they continually mocked God and rebelled against Him. So God appointed the king of the Babylonians, King Nebuchadnezzar, to overtake and enslave the Jewish people. The Babylonians were written about in Scripture as evil people who did not follow the one true God. To have these people overtake "God's people" would have been especially heartbreaking for every Jewish believer.

Can you imagine what Daniel, Hananiah, Mishael, and Azariah must have been feeling? The God they follow had seemingly abandoned them. It seemed that God wasn't keeping up with His end of the bargain. They'd been taken from all that was familiar-- their home, their land, their families, their traditions, their religious customs--and they became slaves to an ungodly king and evil kingdom. The temple, where God dwelled and where they practiced their faith, had been destroyed. They must have been feeling shocked, upset with God, frightened, and angry towards their captors. How could they possibly carry on emotionally, continue to live out their faith, or even consider representing God's love and message to those around them? Yet, that's exactly what they did.

Holiness: Not of this World

In Babylon, Daniel and his friends were given the role of being in the king's service. They went into training so that they were physically and intellectually fit for this service. For three years they had to learn the language, literature, and ways of the Babylonians. Basically, they were being indoctrinated and propagandized into the ways of their captors. This became even more true when their names were changed and when they were required to eat the royal food and wine.

Why did Daniel "resolve" to not eat the royal food and wine, but was willing to learn the culture of the Babylonians and even have his name changed? At first glance, it seems astonishing that he would agree to have his name changed. In the Jewish custom, names held deep meaning and purpose. Names were used to secure the solidarity of family ties, communicate God's message, to establish an affiliation, connection and purpose with God. But, we see Daniel agree to all these changes because he knew names and literature do not "defile" him or cause him to "sin against God."

But Daniel draws a line in the sand that he won't cross when it comes to what he eats. Why would he do that? Because the food from the king's table would have been offered to pagan idols before it was eaten. To eat this food would be to participate in idol worship—something a faithful follower of God would not do. You could change Daniel's name, you could take away his language and make him read your books, but he would not participate in the worship of anyone but the one true God. He would not defile himself before God. His relationship with God was preeminent above all else. Amazing!

So, what did Daniel do? Did he spit out the wine in the king's face and call him an idolater? No. Tactfully, he asked for permission to not eat this food. He literally said, "Please." He was building relationships; thinking long term; behaving in a way that would help him win favor with the people for whom and with whom he worked. Then he makes a proposition or compromise. "Please test your servants for ten days: Give us nothing but vegetables to eat and water to drink. Then compare our appearance with that of the young men who eat the royal food, and treat your servants in accordance with what you see." Here, Daniel is making a pledge. He is saying in effect, "If you will allow us to obey God, we won't let you down. (God won't let us down.) We will be the best servants in the palace."

At the conclusion of the ten-day trial, the verdict came in: "At the end of the ten days they looked healthier and better nourished than any of the young men who ate the royal food." But not only were they better in health and appearance, they were better in wisdom and understanding—ten times better than anyone else. For three years they devoted themselves to learning a new language, studying new literature, and absorbing a new culture, and they became the best workers in the palace. Do you see what they were doing? They were building a platform for ministry to the ungodly Babylonians!

Notice that there was technically no real *ministry* taking place— not yet anyway. No real *impact* Daniel was having on the people around him. Daniel was laying a foundation for a lifetime of ministry and God was definitely working behind the scenes. God was the one that delivered and ordained for the Jewish people to be overtaken by an ungodly king and nation. This God-ordained discipline is hard to understand but is further proof of God's love for his people, like fatherly love. And God is continuing to work behind the scenes for His glory. God is the one who caused the Babylonian official to show favor and compassion to Daniel. God is the one who provided the physical nourishment Daniel needed during his test. God is the one who provided understanding for them about all kinds of earthly literature. And God will be the one who gives Daniel supernatural understanding of visions and dreams.

Jesus in Daniel 1

We know now, from the New Testament, that Jesus is the source of all knowledge and understanding. Daniel and his friends received knowledge and understanding of all kinds from God, but we now receive it all fully from Christ. "My goal is that they may be encouraged in heart and united in love, so that they may have the full riches of complete understanding, in order that they may know the mystery of God, namely, Christ, in whom are hidden all the treasures of wisdom and knowledge" (Colossians 2:2-3). Want to know more about God? —seek Christ. Want to know more about being disciplined in your studies? —seek Christ. Want to know wisdom for your future? —seek Christ.

The way Daniel and his friends lived in chapter one, and the chapters to follow, was a clear example of what Jesus prayed for his followers in John 17:15-18. Jesus prayed that his followers would be holy and protected from the evil one. And he prayed that they would be sent into the world as messengers of God, like Christ was sent into the world. Daniel did all of these things. He chose not to defile himself; he lives in their world, learns their language and teachings, yet he represents godliness to the ungodly officials.

Jesus wants the same for you. He wants you to walk with God because He is worthy of our lives. He wants you to live a life of holiness, because you have been set apart by God to walk in a manner that is worthy of Him. He wants you to pursue self-sacrificing loving friendships with non-Christians because all people bear His image. And He wants you to represent Him to the people around you, because everyone deserves to hear about the great and loving message of salvation from God in Christ. The focus of Daniel's ministry is to see the praises of God declared throughout the earth. As we will see, through patient incremental steps, this is achieved at a level Daniel couldn't have dreamed or imagined. The same goal ought to be in our hearts, for we are "a chosen people…God's special possession, that you may declare the praises of him who called you out of darkness into his wonderful light" (1 Peter 2:9).

Daniel 2

¹In the second year of his reign, Nebuchadnezzar had dreams; his mind was troubled and he could not sleep. ²So the king summoned the magicians, enchanters, sorcerers and astrologers to tell him what he had dreamed. When they came in and stood before the king, ³he said to them, "I have had a dream that troubles me and I want to know what it means."

⁴Then the astrologers answered the king, "May the king live forever! Tell your servants the dream, and we will interpret it."

⁵The king replied to the astrologers, "This is what I have firmly decided: If you do not tell me what my dream was and interpret it, I will have you cut into pieces and your houses turned into piles of rubble. ⁶But if you tell me the dream and explain it, you will receive from me gifts and rewards and great honor. So tell me the dream and interpret it for me."

⁷Once more they replied, "Let the king tell his servants the dream, and we will interpret it."

⁸Then the king answered, "I am certain that you are trying to gain time, because you realize that this is what I have firmly decided: ⁹If you do not tell me the dream, there is only one penalty for you. You have conspired to tell me misleading and wicked things, hoping the situation will change. So then, tell me the dream, and I will know that you can interpret it for me."

¹⁰The astrologers answered the king, "There is no one on earth who can do what the king asks! No king, however great and mighty, has ever asked such a thing of any magician or enchanter or astrologer. ¹¹What the king asks is too difficult. No one

can reveal it to the king except the gods, and they do not live among humans."

¹²This made the king so angry and furious that he ordered the execution of all the wise men of Babylon. ¹³So the decree was issued to put the wise men to death, and men were sent to look for Daniel and his friends to put them to death.

¹⁴When Arioch, the commander of the king's guard, had gone out to put to death the wise men of Babylon, Daniel spoke to him with wisdom and tact. ¹⁵He asked the king's officer, "Why did the king issue such a harsh decree?" Arioch then explained the matter to Daniel. ¹⁶At this, Daniel went in to the king and asked for time, so that he might interpret the dream for him.

¹⁷Then Daniel returned to his house and explained the matter to his friends Hananiah, Mishael and Azariah. ¹⁸He urged them to plead for mercy from the God of heaven concerning this mystery, so that he and his friends might not be executed with the rest of the wise men of Babylon. ¹⁹During the night the mystery was revealed to Daniel in a vision. Then Daniel praised the God of heaven ²⁰and said:

"Praise be to the name of God for ever and ever;
wisdom and power are his.
²¹He changes times and seasons;
he deposes kings and raises up others.
He gives wisdom to the wise
and knowledge to the discerning.
²²He reveals deep and hidden things;
he knows what lies in darkness,
and light dwells with him.
²³I thank and praise you, God of my ancestors:
You have given me wisdom and power,

you have made known to me what we asked of you,
you have made known to us the dream of the king."

24Then Daniel went to Arioch, whom the king had appointed to execute the wise men of Babylon, and said to him, "Do not execute the wise men of Babylon. Take me to the king, and I will interpret his dream for him."

25Arioch took Daniel to the king at once and said, "I have found a man among the exiles from Judah who can tell the king what his dream means."

26The king asked Daniel (also called Belteshazzar), "Are you able to tell me what I saw in my dream and interpret it?"

27Daniel replied, "No wise man, enchanter, magician or diviner can explain to the king the mystery he has asked about, **28**but there is a God in heaven who reveals mysteries. He has shown King Nebuchadnezzar what will happen in days to come. Your dream and the visions that passed through your mind as you were lying in bed are these:

29"As Your Majesty was lying there, your mind turned to things to come, and the revealer of mysteries showed you what is going to happen. **30**As for me, this mystery has been revealed to me, not because I have greater wisdom than anyone else alive, but so that Your Majesty may know the interpretation and that you may understand what went through your mind.

31"Your Majesty looked, and there before you stood a large statue—an enormous, dazzling statue, awesome in appearance. **32**The head of the statue was made of pure gold, its chest and arms of silver, its belly and thighs of bronze, **33**its legs of iron, its feet partly of iron and partly of baked clay. **34**While you were watching, a rock was cut out, but not by human hands. It struck the statue on its feet of iron and clay and smashed them. ³⁵Then the iron, the clay, the bronze, the silver and the gold were all broken to pieces and became like chaff on a threshing floor in the summer. The wind swept them away without leaving a trace. But the rock that struck the statue became a huge mountain and filled the whole earth.

³⁶"This was the dream, and now we will interpret it to the king. ³⁷Your Majesty, you are the king of kings. The God of heaven has given you dominion and power and might and glory; ³⁸in your hands he has placed all mankind and the beasts of the field and the birds in the sky. Wherever they live, he has made you ruler over them all. You are that head of gold.

³⁹"After you, another kingdom will arise, inferior to yours. Next, a third kingdom, one of bronze, will rule over the whole earth. ⁴⁰Finally, there will be a fourth kingdom, strong as iron—for iron breaks and smashes everything—and as iron breaks things to pieces, so it will crush and break all the others. ⁴¹Just as you saw that the feet and toes were partly of baked clay and partly of iron, so this will be a divided kingdom; yet it will have some of the strength of iron in it, even as you saw iron mixed with clay. ⁴²As the toes were partly iron and partly clay, so this kingdom will be partly strong and partly brittle. ⁴³And just as you saw the iron mixed with baked clay, so the people will be a mixture and will not remain united, any more than iron mixes with clay.

⁴⁴"In the time of those kings, the God of heaven will set up a kingdom that will never be destroyed, nor will it be left to another people. It will crush all those kingdoms and bring them to an end, but it will itself endure forever. ⁴⁵This is the meaning of the vision of the rock cut out of a mountain, but not by human

hands—a rock that broke the iron, the bronze, the clay, the silver and the gold to pieces.

"The great God has shown the king what will take place in the future. The dream is true and its interpretation is trustworthy."

[46]Then King Nebuchadnezzar fell prostrate before Daniel and paid him honor and ordered that an offering and incense be presented to him. [47]The king said to Daniel, "Surely your God is the God of gods and the Lord of kings and a revealer of mysteries, for you were able to reveal this mystery."

[48]Then the king placed Daniel in a high position and lavished many gifts on him. He made him ruler over the entire province of Babylon and placed him in charge of all its wise men. [49]Moreover, at Daniel's request the king appointed Shadrach, Meshach and Abednego administrators over the province of Babylon, while Daniel himself remained at the royal court.

Introduction

In last week's study, we saw Daniel and his friends living out their faith boldly in a challenging anti-God world. They pursued holiness, a dependence on God, and loving relationships with their non-believing captors in order to be representatives of God. This week, we'll see all of these qualities and strategies magnified ten-fold. As Daniel and his friends faced imminent death, they depended on God and represented God to those around them. In addition, their witness began to pull the heart of a king towards knowing the one true God. It's a radical story filled with desperation and dependence, humility and boldness, love and hard truth. May this story become how we live out a supernatural faith in this natural world.

Discussion Questions

1. What are the key points to remember from Chapter 1? How did Daniel and his friends live not of the world, but sent into the world in Chapter 1?

Read vv. 1-23

2. Summarize the key things that are happening in this passage. Describe these in your own words.

3. Why did King Nebuchadnezzar demand that the wise men recount the dream itself, as well as explain its meaning?

4. Why were Daniel and his friends included in the execution order? How do you think they were feeling about themselves and about God?

5. *Apply:* Do difficult circumstances make you wonder if you are out of God's will or if you can trust God? Why do you think God allows us to be in difficult situations?

6. How does Daniel speak with the commander of the king's guard and with the king? How does this give us insight into how Daniel treated his "ungodly superiors?"

7. What are the things Daniel does in response to the execution order? Through his response, what do we learn about Daniel's walk with God?

8. What do we learn about the characteristics of God from this passage?

Read vv. 24-49

9. In your own words, summarize the dream and Daniel's interpretation. What do we learn about King Nebuchadnezzar's kingdom?

10. How did Daniel treat the king? How did he show humility, respect, and kindness toward King Nebuchadnezzar?

11. What do you think the rock that breaks the statue represents? What kingdom do you think Daniel referenced in verse 44? (For more information, look at Matthew 21:42-44, 1 Corinthians 10:4, 1 Peter 2:4-8)

12. *Apply:* If Jesus is the Rock and King of the kingdom that will never be destroyed, how should that affect the way you live and think today and this week?

13. What stands out about how Daniel talked with the king about God?

14. What are all the reasons why God gave the answers to Daniel about the dream and interpretation?

15. Notice the effect the four friends were having on Nebuchadnezzar. What do you think he meant in v. 47? Do you think Nebuchadnezzar had become a genuine follower of God? Why or why not?

16. *Apply:* How did Daniel prioritize "not going it alone" while walking with God and proclaiming God's message? How can you prioritize godly friendships in your life?

17. *Apply:* Do you genuinely believe God has sent you into certain places, friendships, and circumstances in order to tell others about a "God in heaven who reveals..."? In what ways can you prioritize being used by God to proclaim his message to those around you?

Considerations & Synopsis

As chapter 2 opens, King Nebuchadnezzar has awoken from a frightening dream, and he wants to know what it means. So, he summoned those who claim to be able to reveal such things and demanded that they not only tell him the meaning of the dream but recount its actual content first. It's a brilliant move on his part, because he suspected that those officials fawning around him were deceivers using sleight of hand tricks, and indeed they were. Before hearing their interpretations, which are unverifiable, he wanted to know if they really did have the ability to discern mysteries and tell him what he dreamed to prove it. Clearly, they didn't have that ability, so they stuttered and stammered and stalled for time.

In response, Nebuchadnezzar, in his characteristic rage and excess, demanded that all the wise men be killed. Guess who was included among the wise men? Daniel, Hananiah, Mishael, and Azariah. The ironic thing is that they never would have been in this predicament if God hadn't given them wisdom, favor, and understanding during their training to serve the king. They were promoted to the position of "wise men" because of God's favor on their lives. Because they were trusting God, trying to live for His glory and trying to pursue holiness, they found themselves in a situation where they were destined to be killed. How would you feel if you were in their shoes? Disappointed in God? Panicked? Confused by His plans? Angered for being put in this situation?

Relationship with God and with Others

But Daniel didn't live out any of those negative thoughts about God. Instead, he spoke with "wisdom and tact" toward the commander of the king's guard who was about to kill him. Talk about pressure—Daniel was about to be killed and he spoke with prudence, discretion, and discernment. Daniel likely had a prior friendship with Arioch for Arioch to even listen to Daniel, because he was supposed to kill Daniel and all the wise men immediately. Furthermore, Daniel used wisdom and boldness to ask the king for "time." He didn't demand his life be spared or beg for mercy; he just asked for more time (to ultimately seek God for answers).

Daniel and his friends did all they could do: they pleaded to God for mercy and asked for His help. There was absolutely nothing they could do to save themselves. Their hope was in God. In response, God did something miraculous. He gave Daniel the same dream that the king had. Can you imagine? That kind of thing just doesn't happen. But it did. Daniel, appropriately, responded with praise toward the God who provides! He declares God to have wisdom and power; God is the one who changes times and seasons, disposes of kings, gives wisdom, and reveals mysteries.

Quick side note: What a wonderful example for us to follow in our walk with God! Seek God with all our hearts, pleading with him in prayer to provide and answer. Then, when he inevitably does provide—spend time in praise, thanksgiving, and gratitude. Sadly, I seem to always just remember one of those two things. I may, for a season, be faithful in prayer but when God answers, I quickly move on to action, forgetting to spend time in gratitude. Or, I'll have seasons of not seeking and asking God, but when all kinds of blessings and direction occurs from God, I thank him for that. But why can't it be both? Petitioning God. Gratitude towards God. Daniel gives us both as a great model to follow in our prayer lives.

Four Kingdoms: Jesus our Rock

Back to the dream: The dream involved Nebuchadnezzar's kingdom and three earthly kingdoms that would follow it. The first kingdom is made of gold, representing King Nebuchadnezzar's kingdom. Daniel was keen to make clear that King Nebuchadnezzar only has dominion and power because it is the God of heaven who has given it to him (v. 37). Ironically, as we'll see in chapter three with the Idol of Gold, it seems King Nebuchadnezzar only heard about the part where he was a head of gold. He forgot the rest of the message: with each passing kingdom comes diminished glory, but increased strength. Sometime during the fourth kingdom, another kingdom will come and destroy all the others, fill the earth, and endure forever. This final kingdom is like that of a "rock" made not by humans' hands that will crush all the other kingdoms. Any guesses what this powerful kingdom is?

Most biblical scholars conclude that this final kingdom is a proclamation about the kingdom of Christ. Jesus is our rock that our foundation is built on! "[T]hey drank from the spiritual rock that accompanied them, and that rock was Christ" (1 Corinthians 10:4). Jesus is the king of the kingdom that will endure forever. Jesus' kingdom has and will fill the entire earth. Jesus' kingdom has all authority, power, and majesty...more than any kingdom of the past. What's even crazier, now the followers of Christ become like little rocks who represent the ultimate Rock of this new kingdom. Wow! "As you come to him, the living Stone—rejected by humans but chosen by God and precious to him— you also, like living stones, are being built into a spiritual house to be a holy priesthood, offering spiritual sacrifices acceptable to God through Jesus Christ" (1 Peter 2:4-5). These truths should radically impact the way that Christians (little Christs, or little Rocks) live day to day.

Lastly, observe the effects of God revealing these mysteries to Daniel. There are three specific reasons that God provided the answers to the dream and interpretation. One, to save the lives of Daniel, Hananiah, Mishael, and Azariah (v. 18); two, to reveal the glory of God (vv. 20-23, 47); and three, so that Nebuchadnezzar would know and understand the meaning of the dream (v. 30). Furthermore, notice the impact it had on the king personally. This pagan, wicked king, exclaimed, "Surely your God is the God of gods and the Lord of kings and a revealer of mysteries, for you were able to reveal this mystery." It's not a personal declaration of faith in God as his own God, but it is an evidence that he was beginning to see the "God of Israel" in a different light.

Ministry in the real world is often slow, incremental, and challenging. Daniel and his friends were patient and bold. They personally walked closely with God in prayer and boldly proclaimed His message as God guided. Over the course of their lives, God would use them to do extraordinary things. And he'll do the same with you. But your first step needs to be walking with our God which leads you to pursue holiness. Then, develop caring relationships with non-Christians and be wisely bold about proclaiming Christ's message. God will use your faithfulness to do amazing things in everyone's lives.

Daniel 3

¹King Nebuchadnezzar made an image of gold, sixty cubits high and six cubits wide, and set it up on the plain of Dura in the province of Babylon. ²He then summoned the satraps, prefects, governors, advisers, treasurers, judges, magistrates and all the other provincial officials to come to the dedication of the image he had set up. ³So the satraps, prefects, governors, advisers, treasurers, judges, magistrates and all the other provincial officials assembled for the dedication of the image that King Nebuchadnezzar had set up, and they stood before it.

⁴Then the herald loudly proclaimed, "Nations and peoples of every language, this is what you are commanded to do: ⁵As soon as you hear the sound of the horn, flute, zither, lyre, harp, pipe and all kinds of music, you must fall down and worship the image of gold that King Nebuchadnezzar has set up. ⁶Whoever does not fall down and worship will immediately be thrown into a blazing furnace."

⁷Therefore, as soon as they heard the sound of the horn, flute, zither, lyre, harp and all kinds of music, all the nations and peoples of every language fell down and worshiped the image of gold that King Nebuchadnezzar had set up.

⁸At this time some astrologers came forward and denounced the Jews. ⁹They said to King Nebuchadnezzar, "May the king live forever! ¹⁰Your Majesty has issued a decree that everyone who hears the sound of the horn, flute, zither, lyre, harp, pipe and all kinds of music must fall down and worship the image of gold, ¹¹and that whoever does not fall down and worship will be thrown into a blazing furnace. ¹²But there are some Jews

whom you have set over the affairs of the province of Babylon—Shadrach, Meshach and Abednego—who pay no attention to you, Your Majesty. They neither serve your gods nor worship the image of gold you have set up."

[13] Furious with rage, Nebuchadnezzar summoned Shadrach, Meshach and Abednego. So these men were brought before the king, [14] and Nebuchadnezzar said to them, "Is it true, Shadrach, Meshach and Abednego, that you do not serve my gods or worship the image of gold I have set up? [15] Now when you hear the sound of the horn, flute, zither, lyre, harp, pipe and all kinds of music, if you are ready to fall down and worship the image I made, very good. But if you do not worship it, you will be thrown immediately into a blazing furnace. Then what god will be able to rescue you from my hand?"

[16] Shadrach, Meshach and Abednego replied to him, "King Nebuchadnezzar, we do not need to defend ourselves before you in this matter. [17] If we are thrown into the blazing furnace, the God we serve is able to deliver us from it, and he will deliver us from Your Majesty's hand. [18] But even if he does not, we want you to know, Your Majesty, that we will not serve your gods or worship the image of gold you have set up."

[19] Then Nebuchadnezzar was furious with Shadrach, Meshach and Abednego, and his attitude toward them changed. He ordered the furnace heated seven times hotter than usual [20] and commanded some of the strongest soldiers in his army to tie up Shadrach, Meshach and Abednego and throw them into the blazing furnace. [21] So these men, wearing their robes, trousers, turbans and other clothes, were bound and thrown into the blazing furnace. [22] The king's command was so urgent and the furnace so hot that the flames of the fire killed the soldiers who

took up Shadrach, Meshach and Abednego, **²³**and these three men, firmly tied, fell into the blazing furnace.

²⁴Then King Nebuchadnezzar leaped to his feet in amazement and asked his advisers, "Weren't there three men that we tied up and threw into the fire?"

They replied, "Certainly, Your Majesty."

²⁵He said, "Look! I see four men walking around in the fire, unbound and unharmed, and the fourth looks like a son of the gods."

²⁶Nebuchadnezzar then approached the opening of the blazing furnace and shouted, "Shadrach, Meshach and Abednego, servants of the Most High God, come out! Come here!"

So Shadrach, Meshach and Abednego came out of the fire, **²⁷**and the satraps, prefects, governors and royal advisers crowded around them. They saw that the fire had not harmed their bodies, nor was a hair of their heads singed; their robes were not scorched, and there was no smell of fire on them.

²⁸Then Nebuchadnezzar said, "Praise be to the God of Shadrach, Meshach and Abednego, who has sent his angel and rescued his servants! They trusted in him and defied the king's command and were willing to give up their lives rather than serve or worship any god except their own God. **²⁹**Therefore I decree that the people of any nation or language who say anything against the God of Shadrach, Meshach and Abednego be cut into pieces and their houses be turned into piles of rubble, for no other god can save in this way."

³⁰Then the king promoted Shadrach, Meshach and Abednego in the province of Babylon.

Introduction

My favorite verses in the entire Old Testament are Daniel 3:17-18. So, get ready! First, remember in the previous chapters, Nebuchadnezzar had a dream about a statue that represented four kingdoms which would rule the world until the Messiah would come and establish his kingdom forever. The head of the statue was gold and represented Nebuchadnezzar's kingdom—Babylon. In chapter three, Nebuchadnezzar builds his own statue—gold from head to toe for all people to worship. As we look at the effect of this blatant disobedience, we'll see the opportunity for Daniel's friends to boldly take a stand for Christ without knowing the outcome. They walked with God and their holiness before God took priority over everything else. Let's look at their example of being set apart for God, while also being sent by God to proclaim God's message to the king.

Discussion Questions

1. What is the riskiest thing you have ever done? Why did you do it? What was the outcome? What is the riskiest thing you have ever done for God?

Read vv. 1-18

2. Last week, we learned the content and meaning of King Nebuchadnezzar's dream. Based on this chapter, what do you think was the king's favorite part of his dream? Why?

3. One of the features of this chapter is the repetition of detailed lists. What are these lists? What is the reason for including these repetitive lists in the story?

4. What were Shadrach, Meshach, and Abednego accused of not doing? What was their punishment if they would not do what the king wants?

5. Beyond saying that they won't bow down to an idol, what is especially astonishing, bold, and faith-filled about their response to the king in vv. 17-18?

6. These three men were under the authority of this king, but they chose to disobey his orders. Why do you think they drew a line in the sand and disobeyed on this issue?

7. *Apply:* Despite not knowing the outcome, these three men still walked by faith and followed God even under the reality of likely death. What situations are you facing that you need to walk by faith, even without knowing the future outcomes?

8. *Apply:* What would it look like, practically, for you to be able to say, "I know God can do (fill in the blank), but even if he doesn't…I will still follow Him and obey Him!"?

9. *Apply:* Romans 13:1 tells us to obey and submit to the authorities placed above us. How do you determine when you should obey or disobey the earthly authorities in your life?

Read vv. 19-30

10. What did Nebuchadnezzar do in response to their disobedience?

11. How is the fourth figure described in the fire? Who do you think that is?

12. What impact did their rescue have on King Nebuchadnezzar? What did he decree?

13. Do you think King Nebuchadnezzar now became a genuine follower of God? Why or why not?

14. *Apply:* The fourth figure in the fire is likely the pre-incarnated Jesus. How does it affect your thinking and actions to know that *Jesus* is walking with you through the fiery trials and challenges of life? (Look at Isaiah 43:1-3 and Hebrews 12:1-2).

15. *Apply:* What situations have you been in where you had to choose between obeying God and obeying an authority? How did you react?
16. *Apply:* What are you willing to risk in order to obey God? What is difficult to risk in order to obey God?

Considerations and Synopsis

At the start of chapter three, Nebuchadnezzar built his own statue, or idol, that was gold from head to toe. At best, it seems like Nebuchadnezzar only remembered the first part of the interpretation of his dream in the previous chapter. At worst, it was an act of defiance against God and a statement that his kingdom would last forever, never to be overthrown.

King Nebuchadnezzar required that all government officials come to pay homage and worship his image. Anyone who didn't obey would be put to death. One interesting feature of this chapter is the repetition of long lists. Three times we are told of the "satraps, prefects, governors, advisers, treasurers, judges, magistrates, and all other provincial officials." Four times we are reminded of the cacophony produced by the "sound of the horn, flute, zither, lyre, harp, pipes, and all kinds of music." There is also a detailed description of their garments: "robes, trousers, turbans, and other clothes." It's not totally clear why these lists are used instead of a brief shorthand summary of the people, clothes, and sound. But one guess is that the repetition and details are meant to provide emphasis. In this case, the author is showing that the sound was so loud, that no one could miss the call to bow down. No one. And that absolutely everyone was expected to submit to this idol. Everyone.

Meanwhile, Hananiah, Mishael, and Azariah (in this chapter called by their Babylonian names: Shadrach, Meshach, and Abednego) refused to bow down to the golden image. As the king tended to do, he flipped out and demanded their obedience, threatening to burn them to death if they didn't comply. If he didn't have the authority to follow through, it would almost be comical how emotionally unstable this guy was. A quick side note: Romans 13:1 tells us to obey and submit to the authorities placed above us. This is not an absolute truth. We are committed to work hard under the authority placed in our lives, but we aren't commanded to follow this authority if it forces us to be immoral or compromise our obedience to God. That's never right. Our sin never honors God, even if our motive is to obey the authority God has placed over us. Now, moving on to my favorite part...

The Ultimate Step of Faith

In the climax of this chapter (vv. 17-18) the three men made their stand and said: "If we are thrown into the blazing furnace, *the God we serve is able to deliver us from it*, and He will deliver us from your Majesty's hand. *But even if He does not...we will not serve your gods*, or worship the image of gold you have set up" (emphasis added). Do you see the outrageously bold faith they had? It was more than just taking a stand for God. They were truly walking by faith into the unknown—they'd had no dreams, revelations, or reassurance from God that He would rescue them from the fire. Yet, they would not bow down to an idol—even willing to face death for their choice. They believed whole-heartedly that God *was able* to save them from the fire, but they also knew that God *might not* save them from this death. Yet, they still would not back down from their faith and worship of the one true God! They would not worship anyone but God. And they were willing to die for this action. This is radical! This is inspiring! This is challenging to my life of faith!

Countless stories in Scripture show men and women hearing a revelation or instruction from God and acting upon those orders (Abraham, Sarah, Noah, Daniel, Mary, the disciples, and many more). This is not to say that these people still didn't have to walk by faith--

they did. But these three men in Daniel had no such reassurance prior to taking their stand for God. They knew that God promised to be with them, but they also knew that there was no guarantee that they wouldn't face brutal death. Still, they were unwilling to compromise their walk with God. They were unwilling to compromise who they worship. They were unwilling to compromise their holiness. They were unwilling to compromise proclaiming who the one true God is—even if it meant death. This was a radical, bold faith that I desperately need to emulate in my life. This is why I love Daniel 3:17-18!

Jesus in the Fire

As expected, because of the three men's response, Nebuchadnezzar lost it and ordered that they be thrown into the furnace. He was so enraged that he ordered Shadrach, Meshach, and Abednego to be tied up and ordered the fire to be heated seven times hotter than usual. This killed even the soldiers who threw the men into the fire. But instead of being burned to death like the soldiers, the three men walked around in the fire unbound with a "fourth [that] looks like a son of the gods" (vv. 25). Most biblical scholars believe that these men experienced what is called a *theophany,* or a physical manifestation or appearance of God, and that it was Jesus Himself walking among them. The pre-incarnate Christ appeared to His people! Can you imagine? So great was their faithfulness under extreme conditions, that God Himself joined them in the flames. Truly amazing! [Theophanies occurred several times in the Old Testament (though not always featuring Jesus, and scholars debate whether certain appearances are Jesus, or an angel, or some other way of God revealing Himself). A few examples include Genesis 28:10-17; Exodus 19, Judges 6:1-23, and Judges 13.]

Shadrach, Meshach, and Abednego were greeted in the flames by our Lord Himself, who loosened their bonds and protected them from the fire. We know now that this vivid example is a precursor to the many promises about Christ. Jesus is Emmanuel, God with us, and will be with us through all circumstances. In addition, we know that Jesus will untie the bonds of sin that endanger us. Consider these verses:

> "But now thus says the Lord, he who created you, O Jacob, he who formed you, O Israel: 'Fear not, for I have redeemed you; I have called you by name, you are mine. When you pass through the waters, I will be with you; and through the rivers, they shall not overwhelm you; when you walk through fire you shall not be burned, and the flame shall not consume you. For I am the Lord your God, the Holy One of Israel, your Savior.'" (Isaiah 43:1-3, English Standard Version)

> "...let us throw off everything that hinders and the sin that so easily entangles. And let us run with perseverance the race marked out for us, fixing our eyes on Jesus..." (Hebrews 12:1-2)

After seeing what took place in the fire, Nebuchadnezzar called the men out of the flames, and the three men emerged, not even smelling like smoke. For the second time, Nebuchadnezzar was forced to acknowledge the might and glory of God and offer Him praise. In an ironic flip-flop, he decreed that if anyone spoke against the God of Judah, he'd be cut to pieces and his house turned into rubble. Same wrath, different target. However, observe the second step in winning the heart of Nebuchadnezzar towards God. He was astounded by their survival of the fire. But was he a true believer in the Most High God? Likely not, considering the wrath he demanded and that he still called God, "their God," not "his God." But kings don't bow easily to the true King of Kings. Similarly, ministry takes time. Winning souls to Christ and making disciples is a battle and usually takes time. Patient incremental faith is required. Patient incremental growth is often the result.

Daniel 4

¹King Nebuchadnezzar,

To the nations and peoples of every language,

who live in all the earth:

May you prosper greatly!

²It is my pleasure to tell you about the miraculous signs and wonders that the Most High God has performed for me.

³How great are his signs,

how mighty his wonders!

His kingdom is an eternal kingdom;

his dominion endures from generation to generation.

⁴I, Nebuchadnezzar, was at home in my palace, contented and prosperous. ⁵I had a dream that made me afraid. As I was lying in bed, the images and visions that passed through my mind terrified me. ⁶So I commanded that all the wise men of Babylon be brought before me to interpret the dream for me. ⁷When the magicians, enchanters, astrologers and diviners came, I told them the dream, but they could not interpret it for me. ⁸Finally, Daniel came into my presence and I told him the dream. (He is called Belteshazzar, after the name of my god, and the spirit of the holy gods is in him.)

⁹I said, "Belteshazzar, chief of the magicians, I know that the spirit of the holy gods is in you, and no mystery is too difficult for you. Here is my dream; interpret it for me. ¹⁰These are the visions I saw while lying in bed: I looked, and there before me stood a tree in the middle of the land. Its height was enormous. ¹¹The tree grew large and strong and its top touched the sky; it was visible to the ends of the earth. ¹²Its leaves were beautiful, its fruit abundant, and on it was food for all. Under it

the wild animals found shelter, and the birds lived in its branches; from it every creature was fed.

[13]"In the visions I saw while lying in bed, I looked, and there before me was a holy one, a messenger, coming down from heaven. [14]He called in a loud voice: 'Cut down the tree and trim off its branches; strip off its leaves and scatter its fruit. Let the animals flee from under it and the birds from its branches. [15]But let the stump and its roots, bound with iron and bronze, remain in the ground, in the grass of the field.

" 'Let him be drenched with the dew of heaven, and let him live with the animals among the plants of the earth. [16]Let his mind be changed from that of a man and let him be given the mind of an animal, till seven times pass by for him.

[17]" 'The decision is announced by messengers, the holy ones declare the verdict, so that the living may know that the Most High is sovereign over all kingdoms on earth and gives them to anyone he wishes and sets over them the lowliest of people.'

[18]"This is the dream that I, King Nebuchadnezzar, had. Now, Belteshazzar, tell me what it means, for none of the wise men in my kingdom can interpret it for me. But you can, because the spirit of the holy gods is in you."

[19]Then Daniel (also called Belteshazzar) was greatly perplexed for a time, and his thoughts terrified him. So the king said, "Belteshazzar, do not let the dream or its meaning alarm you."

Belteshazzar answered, "My lord, if only the dream applied to your enemies and its meaning to your adversaries! [20]The tree you saw, which grew large and strong, with its top touching the sky, visible to the whole earth, [21]with beautiful leaves and abundant fruit, providing food for all, giving shelter to the wild animals, and having nesting places in its branches for the birds— **²²**Your Majesty, you are that tree! You have become great and strong; your greatness has grown until it reaches the sky, and your dominion extends to distant parts of the earth.

²³"Your Majesty saw a holy one, a messenger, coming down from heaven and saying, 'Cut down the tree and destroy it, but leave the stump, bound with iron and bronze, in the grass of the field, while its roots remain in the ground. Let him be drenched with the dew of heaven; let him live with the wild animals, until seven times pass by for him.'

²⁴"This is the interpretation, Your Majesty, and this is the decree the Most High has issued against my lord the king: **²⁵**You will be driven away from people and will live with the wild animals; you will eat grass like the ox and be drenched with the dew of heaven. Seven times will pass by for you until you acknowledge that the Most High is sovereign over all kingdoms on earth and gives them to anyone he wishes. **²⁶**The command to leave the stump of the tree with its roots means that your kingdom will be restored to you when you acknowledge that Heaven rules. **²⁷**Therefore, Your Majesty, be pleased to accept my advice: Renounce your sins by doing what is right, and your wickedness by being kind to the oppressed. It may be that then your prosperity will continue."

²⁸All this happened to King Nebuchadnezzar. **²⁹**Twelve months later, as the king was walking on the roof of the royal palace of Babylon, **³⁰**he said, "Is not this the great Babylon I have built as the royal residence, by my mighty power and for the glory of my majesty?"

³¹Even as the words were on his lips, a voice came from heaven, "This is what is decreed for you, King Nebuchadnezzar: Your royal authority has been taken from you. **³²**You will be driven away from people and will live with the wild animals; you will eat grass like the ox. Seven times will pass by for you until you acknowledge that the Most High is sovereign over all kingdoms on earth and gives them to anyone he wishes."

³³Immediately what had been said about Nebuchadnezzar was fulfilled. He was driven away from people and ate grass like the ox. His body was drenched with the dew of heaven until his hair grew like the feathers of an eagle and his nails like the claws of a bird.

³⁴At the end of that time, I, Nebuchadnezzar, raised my eyes toward heaven, and my sanity was restored. Then I praised the Most High; I honored and glorified him who lives forever.

His dominion is an eternal dominion;
his kingdom endures from generation to generation.
³⁵All the peoples of the earth
are regarded as nothing.
He does as he pleases
with the powers of heaven
and the peoples of the earth.
No one can hold back his hand
or say to him: "What have you done?"

³⁶At the same time that my sanity was restored, my honor and splendor were returned to me for the glory of my kingdom. My advisers and nobles sought me out, and I was restored to my throne and became even greater than before. ³⁷Now I, Nebuchadnezzar, praise and exalt and glorify the King of heaven, because everything he does is right and all his ways are just. And those who walk in pride he is able to humble.

Introduction

This chapter opens in a structure that is much different from the first three chapters. If you are familiar with the epistles of the New Testament, you'll notice that this also is a letter that starts with an introduction. Specifically, this is a letter written by Nebuchadnezzar, looking back over his life and over the most recent events in his life. His letter is addressed to all the inhabitants of the earth, in which he gives honor and praise to God. It seems like he was basically writing his testimony of coming to faith. Pretty astonishing! This ancient letter, which has been preserved for over 2,500 years, is the fourth chapter of Daniel, written from king Nebuchadnezzar's perspective.

Discussion Questions

1. What is the hardest, but best "constructive criticism" you have ever received? How did it make you feel in the moment? How did it help you in the long run?

Read vv. 1-18

2. The author's voice and writing structure changes from previous chapters. Who is speaking? What tense (past or present) is used in vv. 1-3 compared to vv. 4-18. Why is this important to understand the context?

3. How does Nebuchadnezzar describe God in vv. 1-3? What did he call Him in chapters two and three? Why is this change significant?

4. What are the details of Nebuchadnezzar's dream? Why was he terrified by this dream?

5. From vv. 15b-17, Nebuchadnezzar's dream became more literal. In this passage, what purpose is given for the coming judgement on him?

Read vv. 19-27

6. What stands out about how Daniel cared for and valued Nebuchadnezzar? Why wasn't he excited to see this "evil king" and "slave master" receive judgment?

7. What are the details of Daniel's interpretation of the dream?

8. What actions did Daniel call Nebuchadnezzar to take at the end of the interpretation?

9. *Apply:* In what areas of your life do you need to "renounce your sins, do what is right, and acknowledge that God is King?" Take some extra time to reflect on this personally.

10. *Apply:* Daniel balanced proclaiming hard truths (repent and acknowledge that God rules and judgment will be on you), while also declaring grace, hope, and love. How do you think you can live out this balance as you proclaim the gospel of Jesus to others?

Read vv. 28-37

11. Nebuchadnezzar was warned of this judgement on his sin, but still fell into it. Why?

12. Describe what happened to Nebuchadnezzar in vv. 31-33. Crazy, right?

13. What changed in Nebuchadnezzar's perspective and thoughts in vv. 34-37? What stands out about how he described God?

14. It's ultimately up to God, but do you think Nebuchadnezzar will be in heaven? Why or why not?

15. *Apply:* When have you forgotten what you know God has said? How can we better remember God's truth throughout our days?

16. *Apply:* This incredible spiritual change in Nebuchadnezzar didn't happen quickly. How does this effect the way that you should view the mission God has on your life to share your faith and make disciples?

17. *Apply:* What can you emulate from the life of Daniel and his friends?

Considerations and Synopsis

The format of this chapter is much different than the previous three chapters. We have a new author (King Nebuchadnezzar) and it is a letter written by the king looking back on pivotal events in his life. He opened the letter with his current thoughts on God, followed by the events that led to these conclusions. Nebuchadnezzar opened his letter with praise to the "Most High God" and talked about how this God had *personally* affected his life. This was a significant change from his past descriptions of God. If you look back at chapter two, you'll find he talked about "Daniel's God." In chapter three, he was very impressed by the "God of Shadrach, Meshach and Abednego." But in chapter four, he no longer saw Yahweh as the provincial God of some captured Jews. He is the Most High God, who rules over all.

Then, starting in verse 4, Nebuchadnezzar recounted his experiences that led to this change of understanding about God. He again told of a dream that no one could interpret. In the dream, a glorious tree is cut down, bound, and abandoned. The tree is really a man, and judgment is decreed against him "so that the living may know that the Most High is sovereign over all kingdoms on earth and gives them to anyone he wishes." God's sovereignty over men, women, and nations is one of the central ideas of Daniel. The Babylonian conquest of Judah was by no means a conquest of Judah's God. Far from it. That conquest was decreed by God Himself, who "gives [kingdoms] to anyone he wishes." The focus of Daniel's life and ministry was to show the glory and majesty of God. So is yours.

Jesus & Daniel: Speak the Truth in Love

Nebuchadnezzar's dream was really a nightmare, and no one could ease his terror, so he called upon his trusted advisor—Daniel. As Daniel heard the dream, he too became terrified and greatly concerned. His discomfort was not caused by an inability to understand the dream, but rather by the challenge of communicating such an unhappy message to the king. Notice the gentleness and affection Daniel showed to the king. Throughout the dialogue, he delivered some very harsh truths with enormous grace. He compromised neither truth nor grace. It is apparent that Daniel was concerned for the king. In v. 19 he wishes, "if only the dream applied to your enemies, and its meaning to your adversaries." The kindness and care Daniel showed the king was extraordinary, especially when you consider that it was Nebuchadnezzar who destroyed Daniel's nation and took his people into captivity.

Like Daniel, as we are communicating the difficult truths of the gospel, even to our "enemies," our motives must be to care for the other person. We must speak the truth in love. Jesus is described as not only speaking grace and truth, but actually being the true embodiment of grace and truth. "And the Word became flesh and dwelt among us, and we have seen his glory, glory as of the only Son from the Father, full of grace and truth" (John 1:14, ESV). Pastor Kevin DeYoung explains this balance in a story he wrote for the Gospel Coalition titled "Full of Grace and Truth": "When I was being interviewed to be the pastor at University Reformed Church, I had to indicate where I was on a spectrum of issues. One of the lines measured grace versus truth. I wrote something like: 'This is a bad question. Seeing as how Jesus came from the Father full of grace and truth, I believe we should be 100% in both directions.'"

Daniel followed this example. He explained the *truth* of the dream's meaning: King Nebuchadnezzar was about to lose everything—his kingdom, his relationships, and even his sanity. This was an act of judgment for his wicked arrogance. These things would not be restored until he acknowledged that God was the ruler of all. Then Daniel explained the opportunity for God's *grace* to flow in the king's life. Daniel pleaded with Nebuchadnezzar to renounce his sins, do what is right, and be kind to the oppressed. Then God might relent his judgement and the king's prosperity might continue. Take a moment to reflect right now on this message: In what areas of your life might God be saying the same things: repent, do what is right, be kind to the marginalized and oppressed in society?

Now, fast-forward a year after Daniel's interpretation, when no judgment has fallen, and the terror of that night has faded. Nebuchadnezzar observed his kingdom and said in v. 30: "Is not this the great Babylon I have built as the royal residence, by my mighty power and for the glory of my majesty?" His arrogance, focus on self, and forgetfulness of God's message was about to destroy him. Much like the king, when there is seemingly a lack of immediate fulfillment of God's promises, it can make us doubt and forget what God had clearly shown. Our fallen nature inclines us to do this, despite all that God shows us and promises us. Immediately after Nebuchadnezzar's prideful declaration, a voice spoke from heaven declaring the king's guilt. For seven "times" (probably years), he lived in a state of driveling insanity. The specific description of what happened to Nebuchadnezzar is alarming: he lived alone amongst only animals, he ate grass, he was constantly drenched like dew, his hair grew extremely bushy, and his nails grew as long as bird's claws. Gnarly!

A Life Changed by Grace

It wasn't until after Nebuchadnezzar raised his eyes (and likely his heart) toward heaven that his sanity was restored. Commentators differ on what happened at this point, but I think he became a true believer in God. He became a new man who finally understood his place before God. In an act of supreme grace, God opened his eyes to see the depth of his need and God's sufficiency to meet that need. So he praised, exalted, and glorified the King of heaven. And to further show his commitment to God, he proclaimed his own humiliation and also his redemption through God to the entire world. Nebuchadnezzar specifically repented of what seemed to be his greatest sin (pride), by recognizing that God is the one who has all power and will humble those who walk in pride.

After years of faithful service, Daniel's ultimate ministry goal was accomplished. The glory of God was made manifest through the changed life of Nebuchadnezzar. But it took a long time and lots of challenges for Daniel to see this result. Are you committed to walk with God over the long haul? Are you committed to share your faith and make disciples for a lifetime? This is a heart issue between you and God. Be honest with Him about your frustrations and doubts. God can do incredible things in and through your life of obedience, but it will often take patience and faithful endurance over the long haul.

The change in Nebuchadnezzar's life is remarkable, but it's not unlike what God does in the hearts of women and men all over the world every day. If you review these first four chapters, you'll notice how this all came to be. It all started with four college-aged believers who weren't just different—they were better, wiser, and more skilled than any because of their reliance on God. They walked intimately with God. They pursued holiness at all costs. They made wise decisions to build relationships and treat people in a civil manner who weren't believers in God. Over the course of several years, God brought numerous opportunities before them. These "opportunities" were often difficult and looked like challenges, but as the four continued to trust God, they not only survived, but thrived. And a king's life was slowly changed. Incrementally, from the first dream of a statue, to the episode in the fiery furnace, to the dream of the tree, Nebuchadnezzar was opened to the message of the Most High God. Ultimately, God intervened to change the heart and mind of a king. Praise God!

Daniel 5

¹King Belshazzar gave a great banquet for a thousand of his nobles and drank wine with them. ²While Belshazzar was drinking his wine, he gave orders to bring in the gold and silver goblets that Nebuchadnezzar his father had taken from the temple in Jerusalem, so that the king and his nobles, his wives and his concubines might drink from them. ³So they brought in the gold goblets that had been taken from the temple of God in Jerusalem, and the king and his nobles, his wives and his concubines drank from them. ⁴As they drank the wine, they praised the gods of gold and silver, of bronze, iron, wood and stone.

⁵Suddenly the fingers of a human hand appeared and wrote on the plaster of the wall, near the lampstand in the royal palace. The king watched the hand as it wrote. ⁶His face turned pale and he was so frightened that his legs became weak and his knees were knocking.

⁷The king summoned the enchanters, astrologers and diviners. Then he said to these wise men of Babylon, "Whoever reads this writing and tells me what it means will be clothed in purple and have a gold chain placed around his neck, and he will be made the third highest ruler in the kingdom."

⁸Then all the king's wise men came in, but they could not read the writing or tell the king what it meant. ⁹So King Belshazzar became even more terrified and his face grew more pale. His nobles were baffled.

¹⁰The queen, hearing the voices of the king and his nobles, came into the banquet hall. "May the king live forever!" she said. "Don't be alarmed! Don't look so pale! ¹¹There is a man in your

kingdom who has the spirit of the holy gods in him. In the time of your father he was found to have insight and intelligence and wisdom like that of the gods. Your father, King Nebuchadnezzar, appointed him chief of the magicians, enchanters, astrologers and diviners. [12]He did this because Daniel, whom the king called Belteshazzar, was found to have a keen mind and knowledge and understanding, and also the ability to interpret dreams, explain riddles and solve difficult problems. Call for Daniel, and he will tell you what the writing means."

[13]So Daniel was brought before the king, and the king said to him, "Are you Daniel, one of the exiles my father the king brought from Judah? [14]I have heard that the spirit of the gods is in you and that you have insight, intelligence and outstanding wisdom. [15]The wise men and enchanters were brought before me to read this writing and tell me what it means, but they could not explain it. [16]Now I have heard that you are able to give interpretations and to solve difficult problems. If you can read this writing and tell me what it means, you will be clothed in purple and have a gold chain placed around your neck, and you will be made the third highest ruler in the kingdom."

[17]Then Daniel answered the king, "You may keep your gifts for yourself and give your rewards to someone else. Nevertheless, I will read the writing for the king and tell him what it means.

[18]"Your Majesty, the Most High God gave your father Nebuchadnezzar sovereignty and greatness and glory and splendor. [19]Because of the high position he gave him, all the nations and peoples of every language dreaded and feared him. Those the king wanted to put to death, he put to death; those he wanted to spare, he spared; those he wanted to promote, he promoted; and those he wanted to humble, he humbled. [20]But when his heart became arrogant and hardened with pride, he was

deposed from his royal throne and stripped of his glory. ²¹He was driven away from people and given the mind of an animal; he lived with the wild donkeys and ate grass like the ox; and his body was drenched with the dew of heaven, until he acknowledged that the Most High God is sovereign over all kingdoms on earth and sets over them anyone he wishes.

²²"But you, Belshazzar, his son, have not humbled yourself, though you knew all this. ²³Instead, you have set yourself up against the Lord of heaven. You had the goblets from his temple brought to you, and you and your nobles, your wives and your concubines drank wine from them. You praised the gods of silver and gold, of bronze, iron, wood and stone, which cannot see or hear or understand. But you did not honor the God who holds in his hand your life and all your ways. ²⁴Therefore he sent the hand that wrote the inscription.

²⁵"This is the inscription that was written:
> mene, mene, tekel, parsin

²⁶"Here is what these words mean:
> Mene: God has numbered the days of your reign and brought it to an end.
> ²⁷Tekel: You have been weighed on the scales and found wanting.
> ²⁸Parsin: Your kingdom is divided and given to the Medes and Persians."

²⁹Then at Belshazzar's command, Daniel was clothed in purple, a gold chain was placed around his neck, and he was proclaimed the third highest ruler in the kingdom.

³⁰That very night Belshazzar, king of the Babylonians, was slain, ³¹and Darius the Mede took over the kingdom, at the age of sixty-two.

Introduction

This chapter is a snapshot of a different sort of ministry for Daniel. He didn't see the same results he saw with Nebuchadnezzar, but he learned the valuable lesson of being faithful and obedient to God no matter the results. As you study chapter five, look at what it truly means to be *successful* in following God. More importantly, I hope this chapter will open your eyes to God's holiness, justice, and desire to use His people as His voice to the world. Chapter five opens with a new administration ruling in Babylon, King Belshazzar—and Daniel was mostly forgotten about by this new king and new kingdom.

Discussion Questions

1. What has been one of the most discouraging experiences you've ever had with trying to share your faith? When you are sharing your faith what makes you feel like a success? What makes you feel like a failure?

Read vv. 1-17

2. Many things have changed since chapter 4. What are some of the major changes? Who is king Belshazzar? What did he do that blatantly disrespects God?

3. We know from other sources that at least 23 years have passed since the end of chapter 4. What clues show us that Daniel has mostly been forgotten during this time period?

4. Why was Daniel needed to give an interpretation?

5. *Apply*: In what ways are you called to interpret the times for people in light of God's unfolding story? In what ways are you called to be an ambassador for *Jesus*? (Look at 2 Corinthians 5:20)

6. What do we learn about Daniel's high moral character (holiness) from v. 17?

Read vv. 18-24

7. Daniel gives a review of the history of Nebuchadnezzar. What stands out about how he boldly proclaims who God is and the importance of how we should respond to God?

8. What specifically does Daniel call out Belshazzar for doing wrongly?

9. *Apply:* When do you think it's appropriate to confront someone about their sin? When is it not? (Look at 1 Corinthians 5:12-13 for more information)

10. *Apply:* Daniel was a messenger of God to speak His words to the king. In what ways are we called to be messengers of Jesus Christ? (Look at 2 Corinthians 2:14-16)

11. *Apply:* In what areas have you become arrogant or hardened with pride? Reflect & pray.

Read vv. 25-31

12. What were the three words written on the wall? What are their meanings?

13. What is the unifying theme of these words? What is the overall message from these words?

14. What are the specific sins of Belshazzar that have offended God?

15. What happened to the king after Daniel's interpretation? Would you consider Daniel's message a success or failure? Why or why not?

16. *Apply:* The common phrase "the handwriting on the wall" likely originated from this passage and means an inevitable result has become apparent. What warning do you think God has "written on the wall" for us to see?

17. *Apply:* Following the example of Daniel, what is a better way to define successful ministry and better motivations in ministry? How does Jesus define "successful living?" (Look at Luke 10:27-28 for more information)

Considerations and Synopsis

We know from other sources that Nebuchadnezzar died in 562 BC, and that the events of this chapter likely occurred in 539 BC. At least 23 years have elapsed since the close of chapter four. And since Nebuchadnezzar's reign ended, Daniel had largely been forgotten. King Belshazzar (not to be confused with Daniel's Babylonian name, Belteshazzar) was now in charge and was throwing a wild party. In an act of drunken foolishness, he decided he would like to toast the gods of gold, silver, bronze, iron, wood, and stone. If it wasn't bad enough to worship other gods, the king decided to worship these gods by using the instruments that originally were found in the temple of God. Bad call, to say the least. These objects were taken from God's holy temple when Babylon seized Jerusalem and the Jewish people.

As his guests drank to the praise of empty idols, a hand appeared and wrote in a script Belshazzar could not understand, "Mene, Mene, Tekel, Parsin (or 'Peres'). He was terrified. Though he had no idea what the writing said, he was still sober enough to realize that when a disembodied hand appears and writes on your palace wall, the message probably isn't good! Once again, the enchanters (deceivers) who advise the king were at a loss to explain the meaning. Fortunately, the queen remembered Daniel, and suggested that he could give an interpretation. It seems like the past stories of Daniel had been mostly forgotten, and it was only the queen (likely Belshazzar's mother and King Nebuchadnezzar's wife) who remembered what Daniel did with the previous king.

Different Ministry for Daniel

Daniel was summoned, and offered lavish gifts and authority, if he would only explain the mystery to the king. Easily declining the earthly rewards, Daniel agreed to interpret for the king. Then, out of respect for this blatantly evil king, Daniel still called him "your majesty." More importantly, Daniel boldly proclaimed that it is the Most High God who gives interpretations and who is sovereign over all the kingdoms of the earth. He even reminded King Belshazzar about King Nebuchadnezzar and how God humbled a prideful king. The text says King Belshazzar knew all of this about his father, the sovereign Most High God, and the importance of not being prideful—yet Belshazzar blatantly disregarded all of these truths.

The three words written on the wall are "Mene, Tekel, Parsin (or 'Peres'). Daniel explained the meanings of the words, and also the messages of judgment they carry. God had numbered (*Mene*) the days of Belshazzar's reign and it was over. Belshazzar had been weighed (*Tekel*) and found lacking and the kingdom was being divided (*Parsin or Peres*) to the Medes and Persians. All three words are unified by the theme of weighing and dividing. God may have been connecting the judgement to Belshazzar's worship of gold instead of worship of the true God. No matter the specific meaning, the greater truth is that God is angered by the blatant disobedience and worship of idols. And that judgement has come to Belshazzar. That very night Belshazzar died, and the prophecy is fulfilled.

Application for Christians

There are (at least) three lessons of application in this chapter for us as Christians. Number one, God is often speaking to non-believers, but they need someone who is a friend of God to help them understand it. This is the third time that God has given a message to someone, and then used Daniel to make the message clear. He explained the dream about the statues in chapter two; he explained the dream about the tree in chapter four; and here he explained the handwriting on the wall. This isn't because God is unable to make Himself clear without help, but because God wants to use us as His ambassadors. "Therefore, we are ambassadors for Christ, God making his appeal through us. We implore you on behalf of Christ, be reconciled to God" (2 Corinthians 5:20, ESV).

God gives us the unspeakable privilege of playing a real role in His eternal purpose of bringing people into the knowledge and faith of their Creator! What could possibly be more exciting!? There are trials in people's lives, events in our culture, even shows on Netflix that carry messages and glimpses of our God. We, the friends of God, need to interpret these messages to the people around us. We are Christ's ambassadors. John Eldredge, author and founder of Ransomed Heart Ministries, has observed that every story that anyone loves, takes its life from the gospel. The themes that our hearts incline towards are gospel themes. Stories of rescue and redemption, of a beloved who is pursued by a lover, or of sacrifice for someone cherished are all taken straight from the gospel. We can come alongside friends and interpret their longings—the things with which they struggle, and even the shows and movies they watch.

Two, God is *very* serious about sin. We so often trivialize His holiness and think our sin goes unnoticed. We quickly use grace as an excuse to do whatever we want. (Grace is amazing, but it's so amazing that it should *cause* us to pursue holiness at all costs.) God is jealous for His honor and will not be mocked. We need to strive to be a holy people living upright lives, and we need to be deeply concerned about those around us who aren't. His judgment is real, and the stakes are high. We should be thoughtful about what parts of our culture we go along with and what parts we avoid.

Now, here's a major caveat that often confuses Christians about others' sins. Don't miss this! Christians often don't want to talk about sin or judgement because we don't want to judge people. Or we go to the other extreme and talk almost exclusively about how sin condemns people to hell. But there is a balance for us to follow shown in Scripture. First Corinthians 5:12-13 says, "What business is it of mine to judge those outside the church? Are you not to judge those inside? God will judge those outside. 'Expel the wicked person from among you.'" If someone claims to be a Christian, we are supposed to judge their behaviors by lovingly calling them out for those sins. For those who aren't Christians, we aren't supposed to do that. Of course, the gospel message includes the concept that all have sinned and fallen short of the glory of God, and we should point out this general concept—but we don't need to point out every sin in a non-Christian's life. We actually shouldn't even expect them to have the same morals we do. We only have these morals because of Scripture's guidance and the Holy Spirit living inside of us (and yet we still fall short too). We can't expect non-Christians to live this way without the Holy Spirit. Leave the judging of non-Christians to God and boldly proclaim the great news of salvation to them. Then, after they become a believer, let the Holy Spirit guide you and them in the process of sanctification.

Jesus in Daniel Five

The third application for Christians ties directly with seeing ourselves as Jesus' messengers and seeing how Jesus defines success in ministry. Daniel chapter five shows us that success in ministry is based on our faithful obedience, not the results. If Daniel had based his success on the king turning to God, then he would have been defeated when the king ultimately didn't. Instead Daniel modeled for us to walk by faith, do what God has us to do, and trust God that He will accomplish the results He sees best. Obviously, our desire should be to see people turn in faith and believe the gospel. Sometimes, however, successful ministry doesn't result in someone placing their faith in Christ. Our job is to tell the truth and to be gracious in that communication. Our job is to be obedient to love God and love others. We should do everything we can to show the beauty of the gospel, but it's God's job to move in people's hearts as He sees fit. In His mercy, He has saved billions, including you and I, and for that we give Him praise. But He is also just in punishing those who rebel and refuse to follow Him. In ministry, we will see both of these outcomes.

Daniel spread the words of God, just like we are to spread the words of Christ. For example, in 2 Corinthians 2:14-16 Paul says, "But thanks be to God, who in Christ always leads us in triumphal procession, and through us spreads the fragrance of the knowledge of him everywhere. For we are the aroma of Christ to God among those who are being saved and among those who are perishing, to one a fragrance from death to death, to the other a fragrance from life to life. Who is sufficient for these things?" (ESV). The answer to that question is that none of us are equal to it. God, however, gives us the grace to be His ambassadors, His fragrance, and His messengers as we are filled with His Spirit. Bill Bright, the founder of Cru®, defined successful ministry and successful evangelism as "taking the initiative in the power of the Holy Spirit to share Christ and leaving the results to God."

Daniel 6

¹It pleased Darius to appoint 120 satraps to rule throughout the kingdom, ²with three administrators over them, one of whom was Daniel. The satraps were made accountable to them so that the king might not suffer loss. ³Now Daniel so distinguished himself among the administrators and the satraps by his exceptional qualities that the king planned to set him over the whole kingdom. ⁴At this, the administrators and the satraps tried to find grounds for charges against Daniel in his conduct of government affairs, but they were unable to do so. They could find no corruption in him, because he was trustworthy and neither corrupt nor negligent. ⁵Finally these men said, "We will never find any basis for charges against this man Daniel unless it has something to do with the law of his God."

⁶So these administrators and satraps went as a group to the king and said: "May King Darius live forever! ⁷The royal administrators, prefects, satraps, advisers and governors have all agreed that the king should issue an edict and enforce the decree that anyone who prays to any god or human being during the next thirty days, except to you, Your Majesty, shall be thrown into the lions' den. ⁸Now, Your Majesty, issue the decree and put it in writing so that it cannot be altered—in accordance with the law of the Medes and Persians, which cannot be repealed." ⁹So King Darius put the decree in writing.

¹⁰Now when Daniel learned that the decree had been published, he went home to his upstairs room where the windows opened toward Jerusalem. Three times a day he got down on his knees and prayed, giving thanks to his God, just as he had done before. ¹¹Then these men went as a group and found Daniel

praying and asking God for help. **¹²**So they went to the king and spoke to him about his royal decree: "Did you not publish a decree that during the next thirty days anyone who prays to any god or human being except to you, Your Majesty, would be thrown into the lions' den?"

The king answered, "The decree stands—in accordance with the law of the Medes and Persians, which cannot be repealed."

¹³Then they said to the king, "Daniel, who is one of the exiles from Judah, pays no attention to you, Your Majesty, or to the decree you put in writing. He still prays three times a day." **¹⁴**When the king heard this, he was greatly distressed; he was determined to rescue Daniel and made every effort until sundown to save him.

¹⁵Then the men went as a group to King Darius and said to him, "Remember, Your Majesty, that according to the law of the Medes and Persians no decree or edict that the king issues can be changed."

¹⁶So the king gave the order, and they brought Daniel and threw him into the lions' den. The king said to Daniel, "May your God, whom you serve continually, rescue you!"

¹⁷A stone was brought and placed over the mouth of the den, and the king sealed it with his own signet ring and with the rings of his nobles, so that Daniel's situation might not be changed. **¹⁸**Then the king returned to his palace and spent the night without eating and without any entertainment being brought to him. And he could not sleep.

¹⁹At the first light of dawn, the king got up and hurried to the lions' den. **²⁰**When he came near the den, he called to Daniel in an anguished voice, "Daniel, servant of the living God, has your

God, whom you serve continually, been able to rescue you from the lions?"

²¹Daniel answered, "May the king live forever! ²²My God sent his angel, and he shut the mouths of the lions. They have not hurt me, because I was found innocent in his sight. Nor have I ever done any wrong before you, Your Majesty."

²³The king was overjoyed and gave orders to lift Daniel out of the den. And when Daniel was lifted from the den, no wound was found on him, because he had trusted in his God.

²⁴At the king's command, the men who had falsely accused Daniel were brought in and thrown into the lions' den, along with their wives and children. And before they reached the floor of the den, the lions overpowered them and crushed all their bones.

²⁵Then King Darius wrote to all the nations and peoples of every language in all the earth:

"May you prosper greatly!
²⁶"I issue a decree that in every part of my kingdom
people must fear and reverence the God of Daniel.
"For he is the living God
and he endures forever;
his kingdom will not be destroyed,
his dominion will never end.
²⁷He rescues and he saves;
he performs signs and wonders
in the heavens and on the earth.
He has rescued Daniel
from the power of the lions."

²⁸So Daniel prospered during the reign of Darius and the reign of Cyrus the Persian.

Introduction

Chapter six is the final narrative chapter of the book of Daniel. Meaning, it's the final segment detailing and describing Daniel's life. The remaining chapters in Daniel are apocalyptic in nature and involve prayers and visions of Daniel. In this chapter we'll see Daniel as a "well-seasoned follower" and "veteran of the faith." If Daniel was taken into captivity in 605 BC, and the Medes take over the Babylonians kingdom at the beginning of chapter six in 539 BC, then Daniel is now likely in his eighties (if you consider he was probably in his late teens or early 20's when he was captured). Daniel had been daily exercising the muscle of faith. And so should we. May this chapter remind us to walk by faith daily, and to make decisions that involve trusting in God. When you are eighty, don't you want to be like Daniel?

Discussion Questions

1. What do you hope will be true of you when you are 80 years old? What do you hope will be true of your faith when you are 80 years old?

Read vv. 1-9

2. What stands out in vv. 1-5 about Daniel's character in his "old age?"

3. Despite consistently trying to love and care for the non-believers around him, Daniel was still despised by his co-workers. Why do you think they were so angry with him?

4. What plan did the administrators scheme up to get Daniel killed? Why do you think the king agreed to this plan?

5. *Apply:* Sometimes following the ways of God will lead to people not liking you, mocking you, or even trying to destroy you. Has that ever happened to you? How does that make you feel? How can you resolve to please God over pleasing humankind?

6. *Apply:* Daniel modeled for us living an upright and holy life amongst non-believers. Look up 1 Peter 2:12. Why do you think this command is so hard to live out? How do you think you could live this out better?

Read vv. 10-18

7. Daniel, despite the decree, went home and prayed three times a day, as was his custom. Why do you think Daniel was able to so easily trust and obey God in this life or death situation?

8. *Apply:* What is your prayer life like? Is it like Daniel's? What steps do you need to take to make prayer the heartbeat of your relationship with God?

9. Why do you think the king was distressed when he heard about Daniel's disobedience and then tried all day to save him? What is the king's evening like while Daniel is in the den of lions? What does this show about Daniel's relationship with the king?

10. *Apply:* How does the king describe Daniel in relationship to God and could people say this about you too? Why or why not?

Read vv. 19-28

11. What happened to Daniel while he was in the den of lions overnight? How was he rescued?

12. What are the reasons given for why Daniel was rescued?

13. What happens because of Daniel's miraculous rescue from the lions' den?

14. What stands out about the decree sent out? What can we learn about God from the decree?

15. *Apply:* If God's purpose for your life is to be a part of making disciples of every tribe, language, and nation in the name of Jesus,

then what do you need to specifically do if you are to move toward accomplishing this purpose?

16. *Apply:* What can we learn from Daniel's story and these New Testament verses about how we are to live, related to the concept of "lions" (1 Peter 5:8-9), being innocent before God (Colossians 1:21-22), and about God's power to overcome any obstacles (2 Timothy 4:17-18)?

Considerations and Synopsis

The last verse of chapter five transitions us into chapter six by describing the conquest of Babylon by a new king, Darius the Mede. Just as God raised up Babylon to punish Israel, here He used the Medes to destroy Babylon. For 66 years, Daniel had been a captive in this foreign land. He was still pursuing excellence in all he did (both spiritually and professionally), and thereby gaining opportunities for influence. In the third administration (and second nation) of Daniel's tenure, he again distinguished himself so greatly that Darius desired to set him over the entire kingdom. Daniel was found to have better qualities than all the other administrators. This chapter describes Daniel as being trustworthy, and neither corrupt nor negligent. And, as we'll see shortly, he was also as committed to walking with God as he ever was.

He was not, however, doing very well at developing loving and lasting relationships with his colleagues (but that's not his fault). In v. 4, we can see the obvious hostility from his colleagues; in fact, the whole chapter is predicated on their hatred of him. They were incensed that a Jew would be placed over their whole kingdom. Daniel was doing everything right: he was a hard worker, upright in all his actions, walking closely with God, and caring for the people around him. Yet still his co-administrators despised him. Unfortunately, this outcome can happen sometimes as we walk with God. Forming friendships with non-Christians are vital to God's plan for your life, but they aren't a guarantee. Sometimes walking with God will lead to people mocking you and hating you. Just as walking with God trumped obedience to earthly authority in chapter three, here we see it also trumps friendships. Daniel is not willing to compromise his walk with God to curry favor with anyone. He's not trying to pick a fight, but neither will he back down when God's honor is on the line.

Serving God brings Persecution

The other administrators and satraps couldn't stand to have Daniel ruling the kingdom, so they sought to bring charges against him. But they couldn't. He was above reproach. They realized that the only way to trap him would be to pit his obedience to his heavenly King against his obedience to the earthly king. They tricked King Darius into passing an immutable law that would forbid praying to anyone other than him for the next thirty days. From Darius' perspective, this was a way to unify the kingdom, and secure his authority over it. Foolishly, he agreed, not realizing the implications for Daniel. Daniel now had to choose between praying to his Lord, whom he had served his entire life, and praying to a man who could neither hear his requests, nor grant them. I doubt it was a difficult decision for Daniel. He went home and prayed facing Jerusalem.

Notice how Daniel's prayer life is described in v. 10 and how we should model it: "...he went home to his upstairs room where the windows opened toward Jerusalem. Three times a day he got down on his knees and prayed, giving thanks to God, just as he had done before." Daniel didn't start praying because his faith was questioned. Daniel prayed after the decree, just like he always did. His prayers were a daily rhythm of his life. And he prayed three times a day, as was his custom. He humbled himself before God (praying on his knees), gave thanks to God (praise & gratitude), and he prayed in the direction of Jerusalem (his prayers were directed by faith to the place of God's dwelling, see 2 Chronicles 6:34 and 1 Kings 8:42-43). Daniel's prayer life was dynamic, consistent, God-centered, and of utmost importance —and it wasn't going to be changed by the threat of death. Oh, that this would be true of our prayer life!

When Daniel was discovered praying, it was reported to Darius and he was greatly distressed. After making every effort all day to rescue Daniel, he could not. He was unable to change the law, which required any violators to be thrown into a lions' den. Reluctantly, Darius ordered the punishment, and had Daniel thrown into the lion's den. Then we see that the king spent his night distressed about Daniel, unable to eat, unable to sleep, and unable to enjoy himself. These details show us that Daniel must have developed a great relationship with King Darius. Despite his co-workers trying to kill him, Daniel had built a great rapport with his boss through his faithfulness, honesty and hard work. Notice, even, how the king described Daniel's relationship with God in v. 16 and 20. He said that Daniel is a *servant* of the *living* God, and that Daniel serves God *continually!* Could my relationship with God be described like that? Could friends, even those who don't believe in God, describe me in this way? Please God, may this be true of our lives!

Jesus in Daniel 6: Innocent, Rescued, All Nations

At the first light of dawn, the anxious king hurried to the lion's den to see if Daniel had been rescued. And he had! An angel sent by God closed the mouths of lions! And why was Daniel rescued? First, because he was innocent in God's eyes. We know now that no one is truly innocent, not even one. But that we are innocent only through the grace of God. Specifically, today, we are only innocent because Jesus took the punishment for our sins upon Himself and credited us with his spotless record (Colossians 1:21-22).

Second, Daniel was rescued to show God's power over lions. If God so chooses, He can miraculously stop any physical death—even by stopping lions from eating Daniel. An interesting connection, however, is that Satan is also described as prowling around as a roaring lion (1 Peter 5:8). We know that Jesus has overcome the devil (a roaring lion) and that He now gives us the power to resist the devil through His Spirit. (We see this described in 2 Timothy 4:17-18 too.)

Third, and lastly, Daniel was rescued in order to show the entire world the power of God! This happened by Darius writing a letter to every nation and peoples of every language in the earth declaring the glory of God. This letter of declaration is similar to the letter sent out by Nebuchadnezzar to the whole world. It's also similar to Jesus' message to the disciples at the end of his life: "[G]o and make disciples of all nations" (Matthew 28:19), "and you will be my witnesses...to the ends of the earth" (Acts 1:8).

Because Daniel and his friends were willing to place their relationship with God above all else, they were rescued from certain death. And twice this results in praise, glory, and honor to God being declared throughout the entire earth! This should be the same for us as we pursue a relationship with God through Jesus Christ. By having a relationship with God above everything else, developing relationships with those around us, and pursuing holiness, we can trust that God will make His glory known through our lives. What greater privilege could there be?

The Attributes of God and Jesus

Let's conclude this week's study by dwelling on the character of God described in Darius' decree to the whole world in vv. 26-27, and make a few connections to Jesus. Darius said that God deserves to be revered and honored by all because: God is alive, and similarly, Jesus is the living one who is alive forevermore (Revelation 1:18); God will endure forever, and similarly, Jesus is the same yesterday, today, and forever (Hebrews 13:8); God's kingdom will never be destroyed, and his dominion will never end, and similarly, the kingdom of our Lord and Christ will reign forever and ever (Revelation 11:15); God rescues, and similarly, Jesus will rescue us from every evil deed and bring us safely into His heavenly kingdom (2 Timothy 4:18); God saves, and similarly, if we believe in the Lord Jesus, we will be saved (Acts 16:31); God performs signs and wonders, and similarly, Jesus was confirmed by God with mighty works and wonders and signs that God did through him (Acts 2:22). We can see that all these attributes of God decreed by Darius are also true of our Lord and Savior Jesus Christ. Let's praise Him together!

Daniel 7

¹In the first year of Belshazzar king of Babylon, Daniel had a dream, and visions passed through his mind as he was lying in bed. He wrote down the substance of his dream.

²Daniel said: "In my vision at night I looked, and there before me were the four winds of heaven churning up the great sea. ³Four great beasts, each different from the others, came up out of the sea.

⁴"The first was like a lion, and it had the wings of an eagle. I watched until its wings were torn off and it was lifted from the ground so that it stood on two feet like a human being, and the mind of a human was given to it.

⁵"And there before me was a second beast, which looked like a bear. It was raised up on one of its sides, and it had three ribs in its mouth between its teeth. It was told, 'Get up and eat your fill of flesh!'

⁶"After that, I looked, and there before me was another beast, one that looked like a leopard. And on its back it had four wings like those of a bird. This beast had four heads, and it was given authority to rule.

⁷"After that, in my vision at night I looked, and there before me was a fourth beast—terrifying and frightening and very powerful. It had large iron teeth; it crushed and devoured its victims and trampled underfoot whatever was left. It was different from all the former beasts, and it had ten horns.

⁸"While I was thinking about the horns, there before me was another horn, a little one, which came up among them; and three

of the first horns were uprooted before it. This horn had eyes like the eyes of a human being and a mouth that spoke boastfully.

⁹"As I looked,
"thrones were set in place,
and the Ancient of Days took his seat.
His clothing was as white as snow;
the hair of his head was white like wool.
His throne was flaming with fire,
and its wheels were all ablaze.
¹⁰A river of fire was flowing,
coming out from before him.
Thousands upon thousands attended him;
ten thousand times ten thousand stood before him.
The court was seated,
and the books were opened.

¹¹"Then I continued to watch because of the boastful words the horn was speaking. I kept looking until the beast was slain and its body destroyed and thrown into the blazing fire. ¹²(The other beasts had been stripped of their authority, but were allowed to live for a period of time.)

¹³"In my vision at night I looked, and there before me was one like a son of man, coming with the clouds of heaven. He approached the Ancient of Days and was led into his presence. ¹⁴He was given authority, glory and sovereign power; all nations and peoples of every language worshiped him. His dominion is an everlasting dominion that will not pass away, and his kingdom is one that will never be destroyed.

¹⁵"I, Daniel, was troubled in spirit, and the visions that passed through my mind disturbed me. ¹⁶I approached one of those standing there and asked him the meaning of all this.

"So he told me and gave me the interpretation of these things: ¹⁷'The four great beasts are four kings that will rise from the earth. [18]But the holy people of the Most High will receive the kingdom and will possess it forever—yes, for ever and ever.'

[19]"Then I wanted to know the meaning of the fourth beast, which was different from all the others and most terrifying, with its iron teeth and bronze claws—the beast that crushed and devoured its victims and trampled underfoot whatever was left. [20]I also wanted to know about the ten horns on its head and about the other horn that came up, before which three of them fell—the horn that looked more imposing than the others and that had eyes and a mouth that spoke boastfully. [21]As I watched, this horn was waging war against the holy people and defeating them, [22]until the Ancient of Days came and pronounced judgment in favor of the holy people of the Most High, and the time came when they possessed the kingdom.

[23]"He gave me this explanation: 'The fourth beast is a fourth kingdom that will appear on earth. It will be different from all the other kingdoms and will devour the whole earth, trampling it down and crushing it. [24]The ten horns are ten kings who will come from this kingdom. After them another king will arise, different from the earlier ones; he will subdue three kings. [25]He will speak against the Most High and oppress his holy people and try to change the set times and the laws. The holy people will be delivered into his hands for a time, times and half a time.

[26]" 'But the court will sit, and his power will be taken away and completely destroyed forever. [27]Then the sovereignty, power and greatness of all the kingdoms under heaven will be handed over to the holy people of the Most High. His kingdom will be an everlasting kingdom, and all rulers will worship and obey him.'

[28]"This is the end of the matter. I, Daniel, was deeply troubled by my thoughts, and my face turned pale, but I kept the matter to myself."

Introduction

The Book of Daniel takes a dramatic shift in chapter seven and continues this way until the end of the book in chapter twelve. The first six chapters deal with the tales of Daniel and his friends, while the remaining chapters deal with visions and revelations from God. These later chapters are considered an apocalypse, when a heavenly reality is revealed to a human, and an eschatology, a divine revelation about the end of the present age. End times writings can be quite confusing. So confusing, at times, that it seems easier to avoid. You know what I mean if you've spent any time studying the book of Revelation. It can be challenging to understand why there are so many lampstands, wormwood, multi-colored horses, golden bowls, woes upon woes, a golden censer, scrolls being eaten, and the number seven mentioned repeatedly. You may feel the same about this chapter when you consider the beasts, iron teeth, horns uprooting other horns, horns with eyes (yikes!), and thrones on fire flowing with rivers of even more fire. However, if we can grasp the meaning behind these symbols and understand beyond them to the greater reality explained, then we would be astonished at this revelation of God! More importantly, God wants to use this chapter to help us yearn for eternity while embracing the purposes He has for us on this side of eternity through Jesus Christ.

Discussion Questions

1. As we prepare for the final study, what are some of the key themes and takeaways from the past six studies?

2. Chapter seven is an eschatology, a divine revelation about the end of the present age. How often do you think about heaven and the end times? Are these thoughts often hopeful, fearful, or ambiguous?

Read vv. 1-14

3. Describe the details of Daniel's dream in vv. 1-8. How are the four beasts described?

4. What are the feelings Daniel had as he saw these visions? What are your feelings?

5. Who is the Ancient of Days and how is the Ancient of Days described in vv. 9-10?

6. *Apply:* If the Ancient of Days is a picture of God, how can this vision of God give us hope when there is great turmoil in our lives?

7. What happens to the beast(s) in vv. 11-12? How would you interpret the meaning of these verses?

8. How is the "son of man" described in vv. 13-14? Who is this "son of man" and what does he do?

9. *Apply:* Jesus self-describes himself as the "Son of Man" more than any other name in the Gospels. What do you think the phrase "son of man" means?

10. *Apply:* If the "son of man" described in vv. 13-14 is Jesus, how should this picture affect the way you live your life in relationship with Christ?

Read vv. 15-28

11. What additional insights do we learn about the four beasts from the interpretation?

12. What happens to the fourth beast and his kingdom? How is the Most High's kingdom described in contrast to the fourth beasts' kingdom?

13. What happens with the "holy people of the Most High" throughout this section?

14. *Apply:* Why is it important to remember that all nations will become like these beasts (destroyed) and only Jesus is truly worth follow-

ing? How do we love & care for our own nation, while not being so proud of it that it becomes more important than God and Christ?

15. *Apply:* If you and all of God's people possess the kingdom of God now and forever, how does that make you feel? How should that affect the way that you live and think?

Optional: Read Philippians 1:21-24
Philippians 3:20-4:1
2 Corinthians 5:6-11

16. What do we learn from these verses about how to view eternity and how to live this life in view of eternity?

17. *Apply:* How can we, as Christ-followers, yearn expectantly for Jesus' return—while simultaneously living purposefully in this life we currently have?

Considerations and Synopsis

Beasts and Ancient of Days

Daniel's vision doesn't happen chronologically after the end of chapter six but takes us back to a dream Daniel had during the reign of King Belshazzar. It reintroduces us to the four kingdoms, much like what Nebuchadnezzar dreamt in chapter two. These kingdoms are characterized by four distinct beasts that terrify and frighten Daniel because of their power to destroy. However, beginning in verse nine, we see someone described as the Ancient of Days who comes to slay and destroy these boastful beasts (kingdoms). This Ancient of Days is a picture of our God clothed in white, seated on a throne of fire, with thousands upon thousands attending to him. When he destroys these beasts, they are stripped of their authority but allowed to live for a period of time.

What does all this mean? Thankfully, the second half of this chapter gives us an interpretation. I'm so glad God knows our confusion and gives us an interpretation, although sometimes it feels like we even need an interpretation of the interpretation of the dream. Let's try to do that here. The four beasts represent kingdoms of the earth that will rule. Specifically, the last kingdom is the most evil kingdom, with a king who will be given temporary authority. But ultimately, even this kingdom will be destroyed and an everlasting kingdom, ruled by the Ancient of Days, will rise. These images could be describing what will happen at the literal end of days with literal kingdoms and kings that are in charge. Or it could be talking about how Satan has been stripped of authority, yet his kingdom still rules for a time until our God comes to ultimately destroy him forever.

Either way, the message beyond the imagery is that our God will one day destroy all the evil in this world. And that He will reign forever as King with all having to bow down and worship Him. We currently live in what is often referred to theologically as "the already, but not yet." Meaning, we already live in the kingdom of God created by Christ's death and resurrection. But we will not experience its full expression until heaven or until Christ's return, whichever comes first. Remember: Satan has been defeated by Jesus, yet still lives in the present age. We possess the kingdom of God in part but will possess it in its fullness at Christ's return.

Son of Man–Jesus

A most fascinating feature in this chapter is the reference to a "son of man" at the climax of the battle between the Ancient of Days and the beasts. This son of man is described as being in the presence of God, given authority, sovereign power, all nations will worship him, his dominion is everlasting, and his kingdom will never be destroyed! Sound familiar? This is most likely a reference to our Lord and Savior Jesus Christ. Did you know that Jesus refers to Himself as the "Son of

Man" more than any other name? Specifically, Jesus is referred to as the "Son of Man" 88 times in the New Testament.

The meaning of Son of Man is often understood to imply and point to his humanity—that Jesus was fully human. This is only partially true. Ezekiel was referred to as "son of man" 93 times, implying that he was a human being. Similarly with Jesus. We know Jesus was human because he was born of an earthly woman, He became flesh and dwelt among us, and was made in the likeness of man.

However, Daniel 7:13-14 points to nothing about the son of man's humanity. It is actually a Messianic claim focused on his powerful divine nature. This son of man is completely divine and given complete divine authority, power, and dominion. When Jesus described Himself as the Son of Man, He was most likely referring to his divinity, as described in Daniel 7.

> "The more sophisticated and important historical insight is that the term 'Son of Man' doesn't merely align him with humanity. It is probably taken from Daniel 7. And if you read that chapter you'll see that the Son of Man is a very exalted figure: not just a human figure but an exalted figure. It was Jesus' favorite self-designation. So, he calls himself Son of Man very often. I think the reason he did so is because, on the face of it, Son of Man is an ordinary phrase for 'human being.' He was born of a man. And there's no offense there: who isn't a son of man? But those with ears to hear could hear Daniel 7, in which he was claiming a very exalted role in the history of redemption. And he meant to do it. 'Son of Man' has the double meaning of human being and, according to Daniel 7, exalted heavenly one. And Jesus means to communicate both of those."
> –from a sermon by Pastor John Piper, April 4, 2008

So What?

If these visions are to be believed, then it shouldn't just affect how we view eternity, but how we live today! If we are facing uncertainty, difficulty, or suffering, we have an Ancient of Days (God) who we can trust will make wrongs right and one day destroy all evil. If the Son of Man (Jesus) will one day rule an everlasting kingdom, we must not put our hope in temporary "kings" or "kingdoms." We are still called to love the people in our nation, even loving our culture and our country—but it must not become an idol that is of more value to us than our eternal King! If Jesus will be worshipped by all nations, people, and languages in eternity, let's live that picture out today. Let's worship God with all our hearts, souls, and minds *and* give people of all nations the opportunity to worship their eternal King.

Lastly, we need to remember that we should eagerly yearn for eternity—even as we remain fully present in our current reality—ready and willing to live out the purposes God has for our lives. Here is a practical way to truly live not of this world but sent into the world to live for God: Philippians 1:21-24 reminds us to yearn to be in heaven, while simultaneously seeing this earth as an opportunity to live for what will last (living for God, loving others, telling others about an eternal God, helping others grow in their faith). Philippians 3:20-4:1 reminds us that we are citizens of heaven and we should live that way now. Meaning, we have all the authority, power, hope, and joy that comes from being part of an eternal kingdom now, not just when we get to heaven. Therefore, we must stand firm in our faith. Lastly, 2 Corinthians 5:6-11 reminds us to desire to be in heaven, but until then, to be of good courage, pleasing God in all our actions, and persuading others to know God too. This is what it looks like to live with an eternal perspective. This is what it looks like to be eternally minded but doing great earthly good work. This is what it looks like to be *not of this world but sent into the world to represent our eternal King, Jesus Christ!*